EASTERN STEAM IN COLOUR

Hugh Ballantyne

Copyright © Jane's Publishing Company Limited 1986

First published in the United Kingdom in 1986 by
Jane's Publishing Company Limited
238 City Road, London EC1V 2PU

ISBN 0 7106 0362 2

Printed in the United Kingdom by
Netherwood Dalton & Co Ltd, Huddersfield

JANE'S

Cover illustrations

Front: The East Coast route seen at its best with A1 class Pacific No
60141 *Abbotsford* passing High Dyke near the top of the 1 in 200
climb to Stoke Tunnel at the head of the up 'Yorkshire Pullman',
which on Saturdays ran as the 10.37 am Harrogate to King's Cross.
How different a scene from today: in 1961 well kept and litter-free
track formation was the rule, tidy linesides clear of scrub and bushes,
and, most importantly, revenue-earning wagons loaded with iron ore
parked in not one but four sidings waiting to move to Scunthorpe on
the following Monday morning. 19 August 1961. *(Hugh Ballantyne)*
Voigtlander CLR   50mm Skopar f2.8   Agfa CT18   1/500, f2.8

Back: Former North Eastern Railway workhorse in the shape of J27
class 0-6-0 No 65819 going about its everyday business in
Northumberland hauling a loaded coal train of loose-coupled
hoppers from Ashington to Cambois Power Station, approaching
Marcheys House signal box. 1 June 1966. *(Hugh Ballantyne)*
Voigtlander CLR   50mm Skopar f2.8   Agfa CT18   1/250, f5.6

Right: One of the most famous of all top link drivers, Bill Hoole of
Top Shed, King's Cross, standing in front of his steed, No 60007 *Sir
Nigel Gresley* (the 100th Gresley Pacific, built in 1937), at Doncaster
shed at the end of the down run of the SLS Golden Jubilee Tour
from London. On the outward journey, Bill had got 98 mph from his
engine hauling a 295 ton load, and did even better on the return with
112 mph down Stoke bank beyond Little Bytham—a fine day's work
just six weeks before his retirement from BR. Unfortunately the
gentleman standing next to Bill has not been identified, but was
thought to be a guard and colleague of Bill's. 23 May 1959.
(Peter W Gray)
Agfa Super Silette   Kodachrome 8

Introduction

This is the fourth volume which the Publishers have allowed me the privilege of publishing to show trains and locomotives from the former Grouped companies in every day service during the BR era. This book covers the second largest of the 'Big Four' formed by grouping on 1 January 1923 — the London & North Eastern Railway (LNER). As with the volume which dealt with the former LMS, to avoid confusion with the overlap of the two companies into one Region of BR the activities of the former LNER in Scotland are excluded and this book concentrates on the major portion of the railway which operated in England.

The LNER was formed by the amalgamation of four principal English and two Scottish railways, and within these pages there are colour photographs of engines originating from the Great Central Railway (GCR) Great Eastern Railway (GER), Great Northern Railway (GNR) and North Eastern Railway (NER). The latter, the largest of the four, had in fact amalgamated with the Hull & Barnsley Railway on 1 April 1922. For ease of reference all captions refer to the LNER/BR classification of engines and not the earlier pre-grouping codes.

The LNER served the whole of eastern England north of London and much of central England, it went over the Pennines in several places, principally to Manchester and beyond, and made intrusions into other companies' areas as far west as Wrexham, just in North Wales, and Stafford, situated deep in the heart of the LMS system.

The LNER was a fascinating railway with a large variety of engine types, but perhaps three points stand out in the minds of those looking back at the Company now. Primarily one thinks of its first Chief Mechanical Engineer H N (later Sir Nigel) Gresley, who held office from the birth of the company (he had previously been Locomotive Superintendent of the GNR since 1911) until 1941 and greatly influenced locomotive design through the 1920s and 1930s. Then we recall the ultimate accolade of his A4 class Pacific *Mallard* obtaining the world's steam speed record in 1938, and finally the fact the Company was by far the largest user of Pacific type engines in the United Kingdom.

I would like to extend my thanks to the photographers who have allowed the Publishers and myself to include their original and quite irreplaceable transparencies in this book and, not least, to David Caldwell of Chelmsford and Roger Hill of Goole for assistance with regard to information for some of my picture captions.

HUGH BALLANTYNE
Eccleshall, North Staffordshire
November 1985

Gleaming ex-works Peppercorn A1 class Pacific *Bongrace* (named after the 1926 Doncaster Cup winner) stands in Doncaster Works yard. This locomotive was built in 1949 and sadly, in common with all the class of 49 engines, only enjoyed a brief working life, being withdrawn in 1965. 29 September 1962. *(G W Morrison)*
Zeiss Contaflex ƒ2.8 Tessar Agfa CT18

Gresley A3 class Pacific No 60111 *Enterprise* working hard on the 1 in 200 rise southbound to Stoke Tunnel past High Dyke box with an up Leeds to King's Cross relief train. This place was the junction for a mineral branch to Stainby serving some of the Lincolnshire iron-stone quarries, and considerable iron ore traffic was generated here. *Enterprise* was named after the 1887 2000 Guineas winner. 16 September 1961. *(Hugh Ballantyne)*
Voigtlander CLR   50mm 2.8 Skopar
Agfa CT18   1/500 f2.8

Sights such as this brought generations of regular train watchers to the platform end at 'the Cross' to see the action. A4 class Pacific No 60034 *Lord Faringdon* makes ready to leave platform 8 with the 6.15 pm to Leeds. This engine was the last of the class to be built, appearing from Doncaster in July 1938. It was also one of the last survivors, remaining at work until 1966. Originally named *Peregrine*, it became *Lord Faringdon* in March 1948 after the Chairman of the GCR who was appointed a Director of the LNER upon grouping. No 60034 was one of the three Kylchap fitted A4s at King's Cross shed, and was regarded as one of the best of the class, being a free-steaming and fast-running locomotive. On the right, another Gresley Pacific, A3 class No 60036 *Colombo*, awaits departure with the 6.20 pm to Hull. 10 May 1963. *(Peter J Coster)*
Periflex 50mm Wray Kodachrome II

Besides departures, the assembled spectators could enjoy the sight of long express trains emerging from Gas Works Tunnel onto the lines fanning out into King's Cross station and snaking over the points into the platforms. In this typical view, A3 class No 60067 *Ladas* (the 1894 Derby winner), by now fitted with the German-style trough smoke deflectors, eases past King's Cross box with its train. This engine was one of the 20 A3s built by North British in 1924 and was withdrawn in 1962. 30 June 1962. *(G A Rixon)*
Pentax Takumar lens Kodachrome II

When this locomotive appeared as No 500 from Doncaster in 1946, not only was it the 2,000th engine built there but it was the first LNER Pacific to be constructed for eight years. Designed by Edward Thompson, it emerged after he had retired and had been succeeded by A H Peppercorn, so the company named it in honour of its designer. Classified as A2/3, it was one of 15 built and is seen nearing Stoke summit with the down 'Heart of Midlothian' to Edinburgh on an overcast summer's day. 18 July 1959. *(T B Owen)*
Leica IIIc   85mm Sonnar   Kodachrome 8   1/200, f2.5

Stirring sight at Hadley Wood as streamlined A4 Pacific No 60025 *Falcon* pounds through the station on the fast line with a down Leeds express. This engine was one of 35 A4s built, appearing in 1937 and withdrawn in 1963. On nationalisation of the LNER in 1948 only 34 engines came into BR stock as one, No 4469 *Sir Ralph Wedgwood*, was destroyed by bombs during an air raid at York in 1942. Circa 1962. *(J B Bucknall)*
Pentax S1 f2   Takumar   Agfa CT18

Above. Except for the motive power, this view of Doncaster shed taken from the north end looking south has not changed much since the end of steam. In those days there were always plenty of engines parked in the manner seen here. Visible are Thompson K1 class No 62056, 'Austerity' 2-8-0 No 90279 and Class O4/8 2-8-0 No 63818. 2 May 1965.

(Hugh Ballantyne)
Voigtlander CLR 50mm 2.8 Skopar
Agfa CT18 1/60, f8

Right. Up goods train heading south along the East Coast main line at Gamston on the 1 in 200 climb to Askham Tunnel hauled by Class

O2/4 2-8-0 No 63945. This series of 2-8-0s was the first design in which Gresley used three cylinders; a total of 67 engines were constructed in six well-spaced batches between 1919 and 1943. This locomotive was built in 1924 and withdrawn in 1963. 16 June 1962.
(L A Nixon)
Agfa Silette Agfa CT18

8

Below. A superb vintage photograph of a new Peppercorn A1 class Pacific No 60127 in blue livery, albeit rather grubby, pulling out of York under a fine gantry of signals with an up express to London. This engine was built at Doncaster and entered service in May 1949 in BR blue livery but did not receive its name *Wilson Worsdell* until September of 1950, so this picture was taken sometime between those dates. *(Ernest Sanderson)*
Agfa Karat   Kodachrome 8   1/100, f4

Right. Another vintage York area picture probably dating from about the same time as that opposite. Here V2 No 60835 *The Green Howard, Alexandra, Princess of Wales's Own Yorkshire Regiment*, in lined black livery, is passing Holgate and another fine lower quadrant signal gantry with an up relief comprising stock still in LNER colours.
(Ernest Sanderson)
Agfa Karat   Kodachrome 8   1/100, f4

A fine portrait of a solid GCR big Pacific tank engine, Class A5 No 69808, seen standing outside Boston shed. These were J G Robinson's last design of passenger tank engine for the Great Central, built for working Marylebone suburban services. Twenty-one were built at Gorton from 1911 to 1917, this one being from the first batch, and another 23 appeared after the grouping in 1923-25, 13 of which were worked regularly in the north-east of England. This engine was withdrawn in 1959 and the last of the class went a year later. 24 April 1958. *(R C Riley)*
Agfa Super Silette f2 Solagon Kodachrome 8

Like Churchward on the GWR, Herbert Nigel Gresley of the GNR saw the potential of the 2-6-0 type for fast goods and other peak traffic work which they both considered superior to the multitude of 0-6-0 types then the mainstay of most British companies on these jobs. In 1912 Gresley produced his first 2-6-0 with 5 ft 8 in coupled wheels and eight were built. A year later a modified version with a larger boiler was introduced and eventually became LNER Class K2. Together the two variants totalled 75 engines. They performed excellent work right over the LNER system far beyond their original GNR territory, from East Anglia to the West Highland line. Here, No 61759, built by North British in 1918, stands in Boston shed yard with a breakdown train comprising some really vintage stock. In the right background can be seen the famous landmark of this part of Lincolnshire — the 'Boston Stump' — the 272 feet high tower of St Botolph's Church, the parish church of this historic old town. 24 April 1958. (R C Riley)
Agfa Super Silette f2 Solagon Kodachrome 8

Another thrilling sight at King's Cross as one of the York-allocated Peppercorn A1 class Pacifics, No 60121 *Silurian*, erupts into life at the start of a journey down the East Coast main line with a northbound express. Note the huge pile of coal heaped up on the tender and the driver in characteristic pose getting the feel of his steed as its 6 ft 8 in coupled wheels bite the rails to gain momentum. *Silurian*, named after the 1923 Doncaster Cup winner, spent its entire short life of 17 years allocated to York shed. 18 August 1962. *(G A Rixon)*
Yashica   50mm Lynx   Kodachrome II

14

In more passive mood at the end of a journey up from Bradford and Leeds with the 'Yorkshire Pullman', A1 Class No 60115 *Meg Merrilies* stands in front of the buffers at King's Cross. This was the second Peppercorn A1 Pacific built, appearing from Doncaster in September 1948, and sadly like all this class of 49 magnificent locomotives only had a short life, being one of the first withdrawals in November 1962. No 60115 was one of 17 in the class which perpetuated names borne by former NBR Atlantics and 'Scott' class engines, whilst the remainder took names of racehorses, birds, and names associated with LNER constituent companies and locomotive superintendents, so like the streamlined A4s the nomenclature was quite varied. June 1962.
(G A Rixon)
Pentax 50mm Takumar Kodachrome II

Above. The purpose of this book and its companion volumes is to illustrate in colour the everyday steam scene on BR as it really was in the post-war years. This picture is a good example of the general appearance of many locomotives at work in the 1950-60s, and you can be forgiven for not recognising that this engine is today preserved and often working on the GCR from Loughborough. Its present-day appearance is so totally different from the work-weary and bent aspect seen here of Robinson's GCR 'Large Director' Class D11/1, No 62660 *Butler-Henderson*, approach-ing Retford with a Cleethorpes to Manchester train. Today this beautiful engine is safely preserved in the national collection and can be seen restored to immaculate condition in its GCR livery as No 506. 19 July 1959. *(T B Owen)*
Leica IIIc 50mm Summitar
Kodachrome 8 1/200, f2.5

Right. Gloomy day at Grimsby showing one of Gresley's large 5 ft 8 in coupled 2-6-0s of Class K3/2, No 61829, arriving at the platform with a local train to Doncaster. In 1920 Gresley introduced these large boiler three-cylinder express goods engines, and 10 were built by the GNR. Another 183 were built during LNER days between 1924 and 1937, the class having been adopted as a Group Standard design. Although prone to rough riding, they carried out prodigious amounts of hard work all over the LNER system on both heavy goods and mixed traffic duties. This locomotive was with-drawn in June 1962 and none have been preserved. 1 July 1961. *(Hugh Ballantyne)*
Voigtlander CLR 50mm 2.8 Skopar
Agfa CT18

Deep in rural Suffolk, one of the Thomas Worsdell designed 0-6-0 goods engines of Class J15 No 65389 stands at Framlingham, terminus of a 6½ mile branch from Wickham Market, having worked in with the daily pick up goods from Ipswich. A total of 289 of this class were built between 1883 and 1913. This engine was constructed at Stratford in 1890 and gave its owners 70 years of service before withdrawal in 1960. Fortunately No 65462, partly visible on the right side of the picture opposite, has been preserved and can be seen in working order on the North Norfolk Railway at Sheringham. 3 April 1958. *(R C Riley)*
Agfa Super Silette f2 Solagon
Kodachrome 8

A fine portrait of a once well-known Norwich resident, Class B12/3 4-6-0 No 61572, the last of the 80 elegant inside-cylinder 6 ft 6 in coupled express passenger engines designed by S D Holden for the GER in 1911. Seventy were built by the GER and 10 more were constructed by Beyer, Peacock & Co Ltd for the LNER in 1928. These locomotives had all the fine features of GER engines of the period, but were not as large or powerful as their good looks suggested — the very large cab and short tender helped create the impression that they were larger than they were. This locomotive was built by Beyer, Peacock in 1928 and like its sisters worked extensively in East Anglia, although 27 did work for some time on the Great North of Scotland section of the LNER. No 61572 outlived the rest of the class by over two years and upon withdrawal in September 1961 was fortuitiously preserved. Like No 65462 partly visible on the right, it is still in Norfolk at Sheringham on the North Norfolk Railway, where it is undergoing long-term restoration for return to traffic. 31 May 1960. (R C Riley)

Agfa Super Silette f2 Solagon
Kodachrome 8

No 60903, one of the many unnamed Gresley Class V2s, seen in very clean condition with the 4.15 pm King's Cross Yard to Dringhouses (York) Class C goods train on Hatfield south curve. This engine was allocated to King's Cross for most of its life, and the train was a regular King's Cross job for both loco and men. The V2 class, designed as a main line mixed traffic engine, was of such attractive appearance as to deserve names, but only eight out of a class total of 184 engines received them. The class was generally known by the name of the prototype, *Green Arrow,* which commemorated the symbol and name of a registered goods service newly-introduced by the LNER about the time the first engine was built in 1936. 16 June 1962. *(Peter J Coster)*
Periflex
50mm Wray   Agfa CT18

By 1967 the surviving B1s were very thin on the ground and Low Moor shed near Bradford in the West Riding of Yorkshire had the last three on its books. Although bereft of name-plates, No 61030 ex-*Nyala*, appears in good fettle whilst busy in this important industrial region hauling a Leeds-bound goods train from Laisterdyke yard. This engine had just been transferred to Low Moor from York, and when it was withdrawn three months later with its sisters, Nos 61306 and 61337, they were the last B1s in service on BR except for those put into temporary departmental use. June 1967. *(F G Cronin)*
Zeiss Werra I f2.8 Tessar   Agfa CT18

In 1945 Thompson had ideas of rebuilding the three-cylinder Gresley K4 class 2-6-0s with his standard two-cylinder layout and a shortened version of his B1 boiler. One engine, No 3445 was so rebuilt, classified K1/1, and was found after tests to be a satisfactory locomotive. In 1947 an order was placed with North British to build 70 engines, but the first did not appear until Thompson had retired and A H Peppercorn had taken over. Classified K1, they proved to be extremely useful engines and saw service to the end of Eastern Region steam in 1967. This engine, No 62057, seen outside North Blyth shed, was built in 1949 and withdrawn in 1967. It had one moment of glory in August 1965 when it unusually hauled a goods train well off the territory as far south-west as Bristol. 1 June 1966.
(Hugh Ballantyne)
Voigtlander CLR 50mm 2.8 Skopar
Agfa CT18 1/60, f8

The interior of North Blyth shed (then shed code 52F), showing three of its usual residents around the turntable, ex-NER J27 class 0-6-0s Nos 65869, 65880 and 65801. Fifteen months later steam working finished from this and other North Eastern area sheds, and this was the end of steam on Eastern Region. 1 June 1966. (*Hugh Ballantyne*)

Voigtlander CLR   50mm 2.8 Skopar
Agfa CT18 1/30, f2.8

Left. A time-honoured East Coast main line scene of an elegant Gresley Pacific No 60110 *Robert the Devil* (the 1880 St Leger winner) near Great Ponton pounding up the 1 in 200 rise from Grantham towards Stoke Tunnel with the 10 am Leeds to King's Cross express. 22 May 1961. *(Hugh Ballantyne)*
Voigtlander CLR 50mm 2.8 Skopar

Agfa CT18 1/500, f2.8/4

Above. The penultimate A3 Pacific No 60042 *Singapore* (the 1930 St Leger winner), constructed at Doncaster in December 1934, looks work-stained with paint burnt-off part of the smokebox as she gallops up the 1 in 200

gradient past High Dyke box with the 9.30 am Newcastle to King's Cross, the up 'Northumbrian' express. This engine was one of 23 out of a class of 79 to be withdrawn in 1964, July being the fatal month in this instance. 16 September 1961. *(Hugh Ballantyne)*
Voigtlander CLR 50mm 2.8 Skopar
Agfa CT18 1/500, f2.8

25

The 2-6-2 wheel arrangement on tender locomotives never found much favour with any of the locomotive chiefs of British companies, except the LNER. In 1936 Gresley introduced 184 well-proportioned engines of this type which were classified V2, and with minor exceptions they were the only 2-6-2 tender engines used in this country. The elegant good looks of a Gresley design are clearly seen here as No 60899 heads north down the GCR line near Charwelton with the 12.25 pm Marylebone to Nottingham Victoria express on a cold day near the end of the great winter freeze of 1962-63. 2 March 1963.
(Michael Mensing)
Voigtlander Bessa II   3.5 colour Heliar
Ektachrome High Speed   1/500, f5

An interesting scene at Charwelton station showing the typical island platform arrangement used by the GCR when it constructed this railway south to London during the last days of the 19th century. The GCR's London Extension was opened in 1899 and was the last major main line railway built in England. Charwelton is a small village on the extreme western border of Northamptonshire, just a few miles north of the once important junction of Woodford Halse. It was the only point on the GC where an ironstone quarry line connected with a main line station, and the siding is that trailing in on the extreme right of the picture. Class 01 2-8-0 No 63784 passes by on the down line heading north with mainly wooden-bodied empty mineral wagons. May 1953. (*J M Jarvis*)

Kodak Retina I   3.5 Ektar   Kodachrome 8

Up to the mid-1960s this was an almost timeless scene in the north-east of England as a typical NER 0-6-0 designed by Wilson Worsdell, Class J27 No 65831, shoots smoke under the signal gantry at Ryhope Grange Junction on the North Sea coast just south of Sunderland with one of many thousands of coal train trip workings which passed through this junction. The NER and LNER built 115 locomotives in the class between 1906 and 1923, this engine having been constructed by contractors Robert Stephenson in 1909. It was withdrawn in 1966. 20 September 1965.
(Hugh Ballantyne)
Voigtlander CLR   50mm 2.8 Skopar
Agfa CT18   1/250, f4

Another scene at Ryhope Grange Junction, this time showing the last generation of LNER designs, as Peppercorn K1 class 2-6-0 No 62026 heads south down the Durham coast line with empty mineral wagons. Seventy K1s were built by North British in 1949-50 just after nationalisation; they were useful locomotives with a versatility nearly as good as the slightly larger Thompson B1s. They could be seen on humble duties such as this through to express passenger workings over much of the system including, not least, the West Highland line to Mallaig. The electric lighting for marker lights can clearly be seen on this engine together with the Stone's steam generator alongside the smokebox on the right side of the engine, which at the time was regarded as a very modern feature on UK steam designs. 20 September 1965. *(Hugh Ballantyne)*
Voigtlander CLR   50mm 2.8 Skopar
Agfa CT18   1/250, f5.6

Above. Portrait of K1 class 2-6-0 No 62036 in spotless ex-workshops condition standing at York. Almost certainly the engine was photographed just after being repaired at Darlington Works, and was no doubt being run in prior to working back to her home shed. No 62036 was built in 1949 and withdrawn in October 1963. Circa 1962. *(Ernest Sanderson)* *Voigtlander Bessa II   3.5 Skopar Ektachrome*

Right. On a cold winter's night Gresley A3 class Pacific No 60100 *Spearmint* (the 1906 Derby winner) stands at Newcastle upon Tyne Central station waiting to take the empty stock of the down 'Tees Tyne Pullman' out to the carriage sidings at Heaton. This engine was built at Doncaster in 1930 and spent its entire life allocated in Scotland. It had once been one of the Haymarket regulars working the summer non-stops to King's Cross, for which it was kept in spotless condition. When this picture was taken, it had just been transferred to St Margaret's (Edinburgh) and became one of the last three surviving A3s, spending its final years until June 1965 on the Waverley line to Carlisle or, as on this day, occasionally working up to Newcastle with a local train from Berwick. 1 February 1963. *(M Johnson)* *Leica IIIg   50mm f2 Sumitar Agfa CT18   8 secs, f5.6*

Cantering down the GN main line in North London at Wood Green is No 64253, a J6 0-6-0 designed by H A Ivatt and built by his successor H N Gresley, at the head of a breakdown train. The J6 was a useful general-purpose 0-6-0, used primarily in the Nottingham, Doncaster and Peterborough areas, although a few worked at the London end from Hatfield and Hitchin sheds. No 64253 was built at Doncaster in 1919 and withdrawn in 1962. 13 September 1958. *(R C Riley)*

Agfa Super Silette f2 Solagon
Kodachrome 8

Heading south from Wood Green with a mixed rake of BR and Gresley coaches is one of the nine designated post-war standard types of the LNER, Thompson-designed L1 class 2-6-4T No 67767 en route to King's Cross with ECS to form an afternoon down train. One hundred of these large passenger tanks were built, with the prototype No 9000 completed at Doncaster in 1945. The rest of the class did not appear until after nationalisation, 29 being constructed at Darlington in 1948, North British building 35 in 1948-49 and Robert Stephenson & Hawthorns producing 35 in 1949-50. This locomotive was the second Stephenson engine built in 1949. These were useful machines but suffered from overheating of axleboxes. The whole class only had a short working life and all had gone by December 1962, not so much due to their inherent defect but the onslaught of the ever-increasing numbers of DMUs which steadily took over their local passenger duties. 13 September 1958. *(R C Riley)*
Agfa Super Silette f2 Solagon
Kodachrome 8

The class which unquestionably epitomised the local passenger workings to the 'Northern Heights' from the City and King's Cross throughout the LNER era and beyond to 1962 was Gresley's N2 0-6-2T. A total of 107 engines were built, 60 in 1920-21, just before the Grouping, and another 47 between 1925 and 1929. All but 24 had condensing gear fitted when new. The locomotives were intended as suburban tank engines, and the design requirement to keep them within the restricted . loading gauge of the Metropolitan Railway, together with a high-pitched boiler centred at 8 ft 9 in above rail level necessitated by the location of piston valves above the two inside cylinders, gave them an aggressive, powerful appearance. Although the majority worked from King's Cross and Hornsey depots, they also operated, among other places, in the Scottish Area of the LNER, in Yorkshire and for two periods even out of Liverpool Street in company with a multitude of their GER coun- terparts, the N7s. This picture shows one place where they are best remembered, with No 69526 (built by the North British Locomotive Company in 1921 and withdrawn in 1959) leaving Hornsey on 20 September 1958 with a down local train formed of BR-built non-corridor stock. *(R C Riley)*
Agfa Super Silette f2 Solagon
Kodachrome 8 ASA 1/250, f2.8

On a bright winter's day a Thompson L1 class 2-6-4T No 67785, built by Robert Stephenson & Hawthorns in 1950, is seen on a typical working of the era. What a pleasing sight it was, hauling a set of non-corridor coaches along the up slow line near Brookman's Park en route to London with the 12.55 pm from Hitchin. 28 February 1959. (*T B Owen*)
Leica IIIc 85mm Sonnar Kodachrome 8 1/200, f2.4

Left. There have always been a few well-known sheds of each company or Region of BR which consistently over the years turned out engines for work in excellent condition. On the GE section Stratford had, and still has, the ability and enthusiasm to rise to the occasion with immaculate locomotives. It was a tradition that the Liverpool Street pilot, supplied by Stratford, was always kept in shining condition, and here is the evidence of the 1961 example, this little Holden J69/1 class 0-6-0T No 68619, which had been repainted two years previously in GER blue livery with red lining.

Note it also carries the BR emblem, and below its BR number on the bunker, the GER crest. It had been a Liverpool Street pilot since January 1948 and was withdrawn in October 1961. 25 March 1961. *(T B Owen)*
Leica M2 50mm Summicron Kodachrome 8 1 sec, f9

Above. At a quick glance this engine looks like a B1, and although the style of Thompson is evident, a closer look will indicate it is indeed one of the standard types devised by Thomp-

son, but is a class B2, rebuilt from Gresley's B17 'Sandringham' class. Ten of the 73 'Sandringhams' were so rebuilt with the same boiler as used on the B1s, the 100A type. Seen here at Stratford, No 61644 *Earlham Hall* was the last to be rebuilt, emerging from Darlington in 1949 and was withdrawn only ten years later in November 1959. All ten of the B2's retained their numbers and names they previously carried within the 'Sandringham' class series. 23 March 1958. *(T B Owen)*
Leica IIIc 50mm Summitar Kodachrome 8 1/60, f4.2

Albeit on down goods train, Top Shed (as King's Cross was known) Gresley A3 class 60109 *Hermit* (the 1867 Derby winner) looks superb in the winter sunshine seen near Brayton Junction just south of Selby. The engine is in its final form fitted with a double chimney and the very distinctive trough type smoke deflectors fitted to all the class survivors from 1961 onwards. *Hermit* was one of the earliest Gresley Pacifics built, emerging from Doncaster Works in July 1923 as No 4478, and was withdrawn in December 1962.

(Ernest Sanderson)
Voigtlander Bessa II 3.5 Skopar
Ektachrome 1/250, f5.6

The elegant design and proportions are shown to best effect in this fine study of the penultimate surviving Peppercorn A1 class Pacific No 60124 *Kenilworth* on standby duty for East Coast main line work at Darlington shed. In the sixties, the gathering momentum of dieselisation reduced the main line work of these engines; steadily there was less for them to do, although this locomotive with sister No 60145 *St Mungo* shared the Darlington standby job from November 1964 and were pressed into main line service quite frequently to cover diesel failures. No 60124 was withdrawn in March 1966. *(Peter J Robinson)*
Kodak Retina IIc 2.8 Heligan Kodachrome

Nostalgic evening scene at Newcastle upon Tyne. No 67620, one of the neat little V3 class 2-6-2Ts designed by Gresley, seen steam-heating the up Travelling Post Office to London whilst it was being loaded at the platform. Altogether 92 of these passenger tank engines were built, of which all but the last 10 were originally classified as V1. The V1s were gradually reboilered with boilers pressed to 200 psi instead of the original 180 psi and became V3 class. This engine was built at Doncaster in 1931 and worked until 1964. In the final years, after the class had been ousted from their passenger duties by the new DMUs, some of the survivors found work around Newcastle on parcels, pilot and ECS duties, and banking at Durham. September 1963. (M Johnson)

Leica IIIg f2 Summitar Agfa CT18 1/8, f5.6

This picture shows V3 class 2-6-2T No 67684 (built in 1939) near Manors with a parcels train travelling towards Heaton. On the left the overhead wires of the short steeply-graded Quayside branch dropped at 1 in 30 through tunnels to the quayside at Newcastle upon Tyne. This line was operated by two 600 V dc electric locomotives until they were replaced by diesels in 1964 prior to closure in 1969. 8 February 1964. *(G W Morrison)*
Zeiss Contaflex   2.8 Tessar   Agfa CT18

Between spells of photographing Pacifics on a succession of East Coast main line expresses, our lineside photographer was on this occasion rewarded with something quite different on the up line as B1 class 4-6-0 No 61075 comes tender first towards Hadley Wood North tunnels with two breakdown vehicles in tow. This engine was built by North British in 1946 and withdrawn in September 1963. 13 October 1962. *(T B Owen)*
Leica M2   85mm Sonnar   Kodachrome II

Edward Thompson's B1 4-6-0s were extremely versatile and robust mixed traffic locomotives with a wide route availability which enabled them to be allocated over most of the LNER system and perform all sorts of duties. On summer Saturdays, King's Cross B1s worked the through trains to and from Skegness for Butlin's Holiday Camp passengers, complete with a 'Butlins Express' headboard, as seen here. No 61097, another North British built engine, is laying a thick trail of black smoke over the Hertfordshire countryside at Brookman's Park with a train of holidaymakers returning to London and their daily toil. 27 August 1960. (T B Owen)
Leica IIIc   85mm Sonnar
Kodachrome 8 1/200, f2.8

Some of the last strongholds of Eastern steam were the Consett coal and iron ore workings from Tyne Dock near South Shields. These ran across County Durham on the route of the old Stanhope & Tyne Railway into the hinterland of West Durham to the steelworks at Consett, 850 feet above sea level. The scene here is at South Pelaw Junction, north of Chester-le-Street, where a curve from the East Coast main line joined this railway. Also at this point, loaded trains would be split into two portions for hauling up the formidable grades, much at 1 in 50, past Beamish and Annfield Plain to Consett. Ex-NER 0-8-0 Q6 class No 63455, one of 120 designed by Sir Vincent Raven, is dividing its load prior to taking the first portion on to Consett. 20 September 1965.
(Hugh Ballantyne)
Voigtlander CLR
50mm 2.8 Skopar
Agfa CT18 1/125, f5.6

Peppercorn A1 class No 60131 *Osprey* comes gently round the sharp curve at Gateshead station and noses on to the High Level Bridge to cross the River Tyne and approach New-castle with the RCTS special 'Tyne-Solway' rail tour from Leeds. This engine was one of six in the class to be named after birds. The LNER had previously used the name on A4 class No 4494 until that engine was renamed *Andrew K McCosh* in 1942, some six years before No 60131 was built. 21 March 1965. *(Hugh Ballantyne)*
Voigtlander CLR   50mm 2.8 Skopar
Agfa CT18   1/60, f4

45

Right. Compared with the view today of electrification masts in place and the track on the right of the former Bedford–Cambridge line long since removed, this picture at Sandy in rural Bedfordshire is very much a scene of the past. The photograph well captures the trains of the period, as A1 class Pacific No 60148 *Aboyeur* (the 1913 Derby winner) comes fast through Sandy with an up Leeds to King's Cross train at the start of the steady climb for 20 miles or so towards Knebworth and the last lap of the journey to the capital. In the background is V2 No 60897 waiting to follow the up Leeds with the 9.56 am Peterborough to King's Cross. 7 August 1961. *(Michael Mensing)* *Hasselblad 1000F* *2.8 Tessar   Agfa CT18* *1/1000, f3.2*

Opposite. No 61954, a large Gresley K3 class 2-6-0, coming south near Burton Salmon with a train comprising emu stock newly constructed at York carriage works for delivery to the Eastern Region. Circa 1962. *(Ernest Sanderson)* *Agfa Isolette   4.5 Solinar* *Ektachrome*

An excellent reminder of one of Gresley's attractive B17 4-6-0s, known as the 'Sandringham' class after the first engine in the series, seen leaving Cambridge with a train to Liverpool Street. These locomotives were ordered in the 1920s by the LNER to supplement the existing GER B12s on the heavier Great Eastern section passenger jobs. With some effort a design was produced with an 18 tons axleload, and 73 were built between 1928 and 1937. This engine, B17/4 No 61652 *Darlington* constructed in 1936, was in the later batch of 25 which were originally named after English Association Football clubs within LNER territory. 23 June 1958. *(R C Riley)*
Agfa Super Silette f2 Solagon
Kodachrome 8

The last of an illustrious breed — in my view one of the all-time classic English locomotive designs — which originated as James Holden's Great Eastern 7 ft coupled 4-4-0 of which 121 were eventually built in classes D14, D15 and D16. These elegant 4-4-0s, known as 'Clauds' because the first one constructed in 1900 was named *Claud Hamilton* in honour of the then Chairman of the GER, became the principal express passenger engines until the advent of the B12 class 4-6-0s. This picture of D16/3 class No 62613, taken at Ipswich, epitomises a sight well known on this line, as they long performed and competently hauled the Liverpool Street, Ipswich and Norwich traffic. In later years their distribution widened, but in the main they remained true to East Anglia on both GER and Midland & Great Northern Joint lines. Here in the evening of her days No 62613, allocated to March shed, makes ready to leave for Liverpool Street with an REC special. In the following October this engine was withdrawn and the class became extinct. 12 July 1959. *(G W Morrison)*
Zeiss Contaflex f2.8 Tessar Agfa CT18

Scene at Doncaster Works, known as 'The Plant', where Gresley A4 Pacific No 60030 *Golden Fleece* is undergoing workshops attention in the yard alongside the main erecting shop, where it was built in 1937. Amongst the many exploits attributed to each and every A4, one of the highlights of this locomotive's career was its rostering by Grantham for the down 'Flying Scotsman' turn in 1949 when the engine was maintained in top condition for the task. Later, in 1958, No 60030 made 13 runs in 18 weekdays on the 10.00 am King's Cross–Newcastle returning with the 5 pm on the same day, and running over 9,000 miles. When built as No 4495 it was named *Great Snipe* but was renamed in 1937 and eventually withdrawn in December 1962, being one of the first five in the class taken out of service. (*J E Feild*)
Kodak Retinette f3.5
Agfa CT18 1/250, f5.6

Resplendent outside Doncaster Works fresh from overhaul and repaint is three-cylinder 4-6-0 B17/4 'Sandringham' class No 61662 *Manchester United*. As mentioned on p48, some of the 'Sandringhams' were named after football clubs and a pleasing touch, visible in the picture, was that underneath the nameplate there was a replica football protruding from the splasher, flanked on each side by the appropriate club colours, in this case red. No 61662 was the first of a batch of 11 (in fact the last batch of the class, Nos 2862 to 2872) built by Robert Stephenson in 1937. This engine was withdrawn in 1959 and none has been preserved. 29 March 1953. *(T B Owen)*
Leica IIIc 50mm Summitar Kodachrome 8 1/30, f2.5

51

With only one more month of service ahead, K3 class No 61907, one of the powerful looking 2-6-0 express goods engines designed by Gresley and constructed between 1920 and 1937, stands in Colwick shed yard. Colwick was a GCR shed situated on the east side of Nottingham and was a major depot with a substantial allocation. When this picture was taken K3s were near the end of their working lives and all the Colwick allocation of them had gone, but K3s from March, such as this one, continued working in for a short while. No 61907 was built by Armstrong Whitworth at Newcastle upon Tyne in 1931 and was scrapped in September 1962. 25 August 1962.
(G A Rixon)
Pentax 50mm Takumar Kodachrome II

Soft autumn light gently shines on Thompson's B1 class No 61376 standing in the shed yard at Leicester GC, coaled and ready for work. This engine enjoyed a working life of only 11 years, being built by North British in 1951 and withdrawn in 1962. November 1959.
(Norman Glover)
Voigtlander Vito B   50mm 2.8 Skopar
Kodachrome 8

Above. On a fine late summer afternoon Gresley A4 class Pacific No 60021 *Wild Swan* sweeps down the 1 in 200 grade under clear signals on the gantry at High Dyke, speeding north with the 2.00 pm King's Cross to Newcastle Express. 16 September 1961.
Hugh Ballantyne
Voigtlander CLR   50mm 2.8 Skopar
Agfa CT18   1/500, f2.8

Right. No 60022 *Mallard*, the world's steam speed record holder, at work on the A4s' stamping ground, the East Coast main line. In this picture *Mallard* is just south of Stoke Tunnel heading north with the 2.45 pm King's Cross–Newcastle train, passing one of the large white distance signs, once a very common feature of the main line, which were placed at appropriate mileage points for the interest of passengers. A few still survive but this one has long since disappeared. It was just over nine miles south of here, near milepost 90, where on 3 July 1938 Driver J Duddington and Fireman T Bray of the Doncaster top link achieved 126 mph and took the steam speed record of 124 mph from the Germans. It was made on the occasion of a brake test trial run from London to Peterborough, when Gresley proposed an extra run up to Barkston to make a fast return run down the bank from Stoke Tunnel to Peterborough. With the tremendous impression and prestige the LNER gained when Gresley's new Streamliner No 2509 *Silver Link* made its 112 mph debut on the first public run in September 1935, and the continuous high performance throughout their lives, this record has ensured that the A4 class will be remembered as some of the finest steam locomotives ever built. 19 August 1961.
(Hugh Ballantyne)
Voigtlander CLR   50mm 2.8 Skopar
Agfa CT18   1/500, f4

Left. A general view of King's Cross looking from 'Station Loco' shed, which was a locomotive servicing point where engines on short turnround were handled and fuelled. Engines on longer layover went to 'Top Shed', the main depot situated to the north by King's Cross goods depot. This picture was taken in the evening looking south-east towards Lewis Cubitt's dual-arched trainshed which opened in 1852 to become the GNR London terminus station. In the foreground, Gresley A3 class No 60067 *Ladas* stands over the inspection pit,

and also visible are a Thompson L1 class 2-6-4T and Peppercorn A1 class Pacific. 20 June 1959. *(T B Owen)*
Leica IIIc 50mm Summitar
Kodachrome 8   1/200, f2.4

Above. A scene reminiscent of the old GER as a Thomas Worsdell designed J15 class 0-6-0 No 65460 trundles north through Brimsdown station on its way out of London down the main line towards Cambridge. This series of 0-6-0

originated on the GER in 1883 and became the most numerous class on that railway, totalling 289. The design was straightforward and maintenance simple, so much so that James Holden, successor to Worsdell as Locomotive Superintendent, Stratford Works, in December 1891 erected No 930 and put it in steam in the amazing time of 9 hr 47 min, so setting a British record for the construction of a locomotive. 25 March 1961. *(T B Owen)*
Leica M2 50mm Summicron   Kodachrome 8
1/125, f2.2

Gresley A3 class No 60061 *Pretty Polly* (the 1904 St Leger winner) in Beeston cutting south of Leeds with the 10.00 am Leeds Central to King's Cross express. This engine was built at Doncaster in 1925 and withdrawn in 1962. 25 April 1962. *(G W Morrison)* *Zeiss Contaflex 2.8 Tessar Agfa CT18*

In bright winter sunshine one of the 1923-built Gresley A3s, No 60108 *Gay Crusader* (the 1917 Derby winner), is seen hauling an up Cambridge train near Brookman's Park on the rise to Potters Bar some 13 miles from its destination at King's Cross. 28 February 1959.

(T B Owen)
Leica IIIc   85mm Sonnar   Kodachrome 8   1/200, f2.6

A familiar sight on the NER was the Wilson Worsdell design of 0-4-4T which became that company's standard passenger tank engine in the early days of this century and was later LNER class G5. Darlington Works constructed 110 between 1894 and 1901 and they all enjoyed a long service life. This picture, taken on a sunny day in beautiful Eskdale, North Yorkshire, shows No 67343 in charge of a Whitby to Malton train, a tough job over a severely-graded line which the class performed for many years. April 1954. *(J M Jarvis)*
Kodak Retina I   3.5 Ektar
Kodachrome 8

Fortunately this branch of the NER from Grosmont to Pickering through Newtondale is now preserved as the North Yorkshire Moors Railway and trains can still be seen at this picturesque location, albeit the track is now singled. In this 1954 photograph Gresley A8 class 4-6-2T No 69861 comes up the formidable 1 in 49 gradient towards Goathland station with a Whitby–Malton train. This class of 45 engines was originally designed by Raven as a 4-4-4T and built between 1913 and 1922, but they were all rebuilt as Pacific tanks between 1931 and 1936 and gained a reputation for being strong and reliable passenger loco-motives. The DMU programme of the 1950s seriously affected their usefulness and all were withdrawn by 1960, this engine being one of the last to go in June 1960. April 1954. (J M Jarvis)
Kodak Retina I   3.5 Ektar
Kodachrome 8

Although the GER had one of the most intensive and heavily-loaded suburban systems in the country, it rejected electrification. Equally surprisingly it did not introduce a six-coupled suburban tank locomotive until 1915. In that year A J Hill, the last CME of the GER, produced a pair of 0-6-2Ts, one using saturated and the other superheated steam for comparison purposes. The GER built 10 more saturated-steam engines in 1921, and after the 1923 grouping 10 more superheated engines were constructed in 1923-24. The LNER classified them N7 and was sufficiently impressed to have 134 in service by 1928. Although used primarily as Southern Area engines, some did work at various times in the West Riding of Yorkshire and the Manchester and Glasgow areas. It is interesting to note the last engine built at Stratford Works was an N7 constructed in March 1924 as No 7999, which became BR No 69621 and is now preserved on the Stour Valley line. The engine pictured here in the familiar surroundings of Stratford shed is No 69709, built at Doncaster in 1927 and withdrawn in 1960. 23 March 1958.
(T B Owen)
Leica IIIc 50mm Summitar Kodachrome 8
1/60, f4.2

At the opposite end of the LNER locomotive spectrum from the glamorous and much-publicised Pacific fleet is this little 0-4-0T. It was, as one would expect from anything originating and living in London's East End, a tough little machine, one of five built between 1913 and 1921 at Stratford to A J Hill's design and becoming LNER class Y4. Their 3 ft 10 in wheels carried over 38 tons, giving a high axleloading of 19 tons, plenty of adhesion and 19,224 lb tractive effort. Four of the quintet were used for shunting the difficult yards at Mile End, Devonshire Street and Canning Town, whilst this engine, which became De-partmental No 33, spent its life as Stratford Works yard pilot. It is seen here at the works, and was withdrawn when the works closed in 1963, outliving its sisters by seven years. 6 March 1958. (R C Riley)
Agfa Super Silette f2 Solagon
Kodachrome 8

Left. A striking telephoto picture of A1 class Pacific No 60141 *Abbotsford* at the head of the 6.15 pm parcels train from King's Cross to York. At the time this engine was a regular seen by London observers working on the East Coast route from Copley Hill shed, Leeds, and was regarded as a good performer. Built in 1950 and withdrawn in 1964, *Abbotsford* perpetuated the name carried by former NBR Reid-designed Atlantic No 879. April 1963.

(Peter J Coster)
Periflex 135mm 2.8 Tamron   Agfa CT18

Above. Another Copley Hill Peppercorn Pacific, this time No 60118 *Archibald Sturrock*, passes High Dyke with apparent ease on the 1 in 200 rising gradient towards Stoke tunnel with the up 'Yorkshire Pullman', 10.07 am Harrogate to King's Cross. Note the two types of Pullman car in the formation, the older vehicles next to the tender are followed by a rake of then new Metro Cammell coaches. The engine was one of six in the class named after GNR and NER locomotive superintendents, this one honouring the first superintendent of the Great Northern. 16 September 1961.
(Hugh Ballantyne)
Voigtlander CLR   50mm 2.8 Skopar
Agfa CT18   1/500, f2.8

Above. At Leicester, one of the principal stations on the GCR's London Extension, stands Gresley V2 No 60963 blowing off prior to departure southwards with a parcels train. On the right a former Crosti-boilered BR Standard Class 9F waits to follow the V2 with a goods train. 18 April 1964. *(Keith Sanders)* *Corfield Periflex III 1.9 Lumax Agfa CT18*

Right. A North Eastern 4-6-0 at a Great Central shed in London. Raven-designed B16/3 class No 61434 stands on shed at Neasden during a layover after bringing in a parcels train from York over the GCR main line via Woodford Halse. Seventy of these engines were built at Darlington between 1919 and 1924, and were regarded by the NER as fast goods locomotives. They proved competent and dependable engines working from NER

sheds. No 925 was damaged beyond repair during an air raid on York in 1942, so only 69 engines passed into BR ownership in 1948. Of these, 24 engines including this one were rebuilt with revised valve gear and running plate raised above the coupled wheels. No 61434, which was withdrawn in June 1964, was one of the last survivors. 11 April 1961. *(Basil Roberts)* *Kodak Retinette 1B Agfa CT18*

Coming through Beeston in the southern suburbs of Leeds on a fine day, Gresley A4 No 60006 *Sir Ralph Wedgwood* is getting into his stride for the two-mile sharp climb up to Ardsley Tunnel en route to the first stop at Wakefield Westgate with the 1.00 pm Leeds to King's Cross express. This engine was built in 1938 as No 4466 *Herring Gull* and renamed in 1944 in honour of the former Chief General Manager of the LNER. 6 June 1962. (G W Morrison)

Zeiss Contaflex   2.8 Tessar   Agfa CT18

Another picture of Peppercorn A1 class No 60141 *Abbotsford,* threading its way out of its home city and near the depot at Copley Hill, coming around the sharp curve from Holbeck towards the points at Wortley South Junction before picking up speed on the first stages of the journey to King's Cross with the up 'White Rose'. 7 June 1962. *(G W Morrison)*
Zeiss Contaflex 2.8 Tessar Agfa CT18

One of the most useful goods engines to see service on the LNER was the Wilson Worsdell NER Class P3, later LNER Class J27. A total of 115 of these robust locomotives were built between 1906 and 1923, and they put in endless hard work on goods and mineral trains in north-east England. This is a typical scene showing No 65809 on one of what seemed a never-ending succession of trip workings from Northumberland collieries to the staithes or power stations in the area. This is a very short haul coal train going from Ashington to the power station at nearby Cambois, and is crossing the impressive steel viaduct over the River Wansbeck immediately south of Ashington. 1 June 1966. *(Hugh Ballantyne)*

Voigtlander CLR 2.8 Skopar Agfa CT18 1/250, f5.6

Bird's eye view of J27 No 65882 from the top of a steep cliff on a spoil heap taken one evening whilst at work on the mineral branch to Silksworth on the south side of Sunderland. This branch had severe gradients and was worked exclusively by J27s. No 65882 was built at Darlington in 1922 and withdrawn in September 1966 with the last four survivors of the type. It had the dubious honour of being the last NER locomotive to remain in service, and was also the last standard gauge pre-grouping engine to remain in stock on BR. Its post-grouping sister No 65894 is preserved in active service on the North Yorkshire Moors Railway. 1966. *(M Johnson)*
Leica IIIg   3.5 Hector 135mm lens
Agfa CT18   1/500, f4

A clean Thompson Pacific A2/3 class No 60520 *Owen Tudor* (the 1941 Derby winner) sets out for home from Leeds over the viaduct at Holbeck High Level with the 10.45 am Leeds Central to Doncaster local train. Fifteen of these Pacifics were built in 1946-47 with 6 ft 2 in coupled wheels to an LNER standard design, but due to the advent of dieselisation these and the other post-war Pacifics generally had short careers and all the A2/3s had gone by 1965. 21 June 1961. *(G W Morrison) Zeiss Contaflex 2.8 Tessar Agfa CT18*

A Neville Hill Leeds engine, A3 Pacific No 60084 *Trigo* (the 1929 Derby and St Leger winner), brewing up in the loco yard at nearby Holbeck shed in readiness for work. 17 March 1961. *(G W Morrison)*
Zeiss Contaflex   2.8 Tessar   Agfa CT18

ALNWICK

Left. A busy scene at Consett, a steelworks town in upland County Durham, which in the changing industrial pattern of the nation in the 1980s has been transformed with the closure of both steelworks and railway. Although passenger services ceased in May 1955, coal and iron ore trains continued well beyond the elimination of steam in north-east England during 1967 until closure of the line in 1984. On a bright summer afternoon, K1 class 2-6-0 No 62007 comes slowly through the yard with the island platform of the closed passenger station partly visible on the right. August 1966.

(F G Cronin)
Zeiss Werra I   f2.8 Tessar   Agfa CT18

Above. In the heart of Northumberland, England's most northerly county, is the attractive little market town of Alnwick which has an impressive Norman castle, and once possessed a magnificent NER terminus station complete with overall roof. This branch came from Alnmouth 3 miles away on the main line to Berwick; after reversing one could travel through beautiful country right up to the Scottish border at Coldstream via Wooler, a distance of 35 miles. This latter section closed to passengers as long ago as 1930, but the short branch from Alnmouth remained open until 18 June 1966. Barely two weeks before closure, on a very bright morning, K1 class No 62021 backs out of platform 2 at Alnwick to run round its train after working in as the 7.50 am from Alnmouth. 2 June 1966. *(Hugh Ballantyne)*
Voigtlander CLR   2.8 Skopar   Agfa CT18 1/250, f5.6

75

Left. A reminder of a once common but often forgotten sight of a Gresley Pacific working a fitted goods train. In this picture, No 60021 *Wild Swan* of King's Cross is near Potter's Bar with an up fast goods train. No 60021 was built in 1938 at Doncaster and was withdrawn in 1963. 25 August 1962.
(Peter A Fry)
Kodak Retinette 1B
Agfa CT18

Right. Just ex-works and running-in back to Doncaster with a southbound goods train is A4 No 60027 *Merlin* near Chaloner's Whin, south of York, making a somewhat unfamiliar sight on a mixed goods train, although A4s regularly appeared on fast fitted goods up and down the East Coast main line, as seen in the picture opposite. Circa 1960.
(Ernest Sanderson)
Agfa Isolette   4.5 Solinar
Ektachrome

One of the most significant locomotive designs introduced in Great Britain was John Robinson's heavy goods 2-8-0 produced for the Great Central. Besides working as front line goods engines on the GCR they also became a keystone in LNER heavy freight motive power. Some were built under government order for military use in World War I, and if this was not sufficient some saw service in China and Australia and during World War II in the Middle East. A total of 421 went into LNER service after the grouping and over the years reboilering, new cabs and different chimneys fitted to some produced eight subdivisions of the class. This engine, No 63643, seen at Immingham, which, being very much on GCR territory always had an allocation of over 20, was built at Gorton, Manchester, in 1912. It was rebuilt as LNER Class 04/7 in 1943 with a Gresley boiler but retaining its GCR-style smokebox. After 48 years of hard work this engine was withdrawn two months after this picture was taken. 18 September 1960. *(Norman Glover)*
Voigtlander Vito B 50mm 2.8 Skopar
Kodachrome 8

A much-rebuilt Robinson 2-8-0 No 63706, which by the time this picture was taken had been rebuilt to Class 04/8. Originally constructed by Robert Stephenson & Co in 1918 for the Railway Operating Division, it was rebuilt in 1940 and again in 1956, the last rebuilding including the fitting of a Thompson diagram 100A boiler, a saddle to carry the smoke box, and a double side window cab. Here No 63706, filthy dirty, trundles slowly northwards on the GCR line near Staveley loco shed in Derbyshire. 24 April 1965. *(M Johnson)*
Leica IIIg 50mm Summitar Agfa CT18 1/500, f4

A striking picture of an engine type which, although designed by R A Riddles for the Ministry of Supply during World War II, eventually found extensive use throughout the former LNER system. This is one of the 'Austerity' 2-8-0 goods engines, nominally classified O7 by the LNER, of which no less than 935 were built between 1943 and 1945, 545 by North British and 390, including this one, by Vulcan Foundry. This engine emerged from the contractor's works at Newton-le-Willows in 1944 as WD No 7503. It was loaned to the LNER in 1947 and when taken into BR stock became No 90629. In this picture, the neat appearance of the type is apparent, only made possible by the fact the engine is very uncharacteristically clean and is hauling a down ECS train of Mk1 stock in maroon livery. This Colwick-allocated engine was photographed on the down East Coast main line at Werrington troughs, north of Peterborough. 23 May 1962. *(Colin Ding)* *Microcord Ektachrome 200 1/300, f8*

Thomas Parker, the Locomotive Superintendent of the Manchester, Sheffield & Lincolnshire Railway, introduced his second 0-6-2T type in 1891. This was notable at the time as the prototype engine, No 7, was the first locomotive with a Belpaire firebox constructed for a British company. Once Parker was satisfied with the design, a total of 129 were built by the company at its Gorton Works or by the famous contractor nearby, Beyer, Peacock & Co Ltd. They became the standard shunting and light goods engine of the GCR, and during their long and useful lives some moved off the territory on to former GE and GN lines. Here, Class N5 No 69262, one of seven allocated to the GN shed at New England, Peterborough, stands in the sunshine at the little terminus station at Stamford East, the end of a 4-mile branch from Essendine, shunting the daily pick-up goods from Peterborough. This engine was built by Beyer, Peacock in 1893 and withdrawn in 1959. 25 June 1958. (R C Riley)
Agfa Super Silette f2 Solagon
Kodachrome 8

The North British Railway had quite extensive mileage in England just south of the border in Northumberland and Cumberland, and this included a branch of 25¼ miles through the heart of Northumberland from Reedsmouth to Morpeth. The line lost its passenger services in 1952 and became a truncated goods only branch from Morpeth to Woodburn, where a spotless 0-6-0 J27 No 65842 is seen arriving with the last goods train to run. For the occasion the engine had been cleaned by local enthusiasts at South Blyth shed. 22 September 1966. *(Peter J Robinson)*
Kodak Retina IIc 2.8 Heligon Kodachrome

On a bright but windy winter's day, Raven-designed Q6 class 0-8-0 No 63429 brings a coal train into the yard at North Blyth. One member of this NER goods engine type, BR No 63395, is preserved and based on the North Yorkshire Moors Railway. 8 February 1964. *(G W Morrison)*
Zeiss Contaflex   2.8 Tessar   Agfa CT18

A rare colour picture of a Gresley class which disappeared from service in 1961. In 1925 Gresley turned his attention to a new three-cylinder 4-4-0 passenger engine, and when No 234 *Yorkshire* emerged from Darlington in 1927 it was the first LNER-designed passenger engine and also the last 4-4-0 type to be built for use on the system. A total of 76 of these 6 ft 8 in coupled Class D49 locomotives were built between 1927 and 1935. They were subdivided into two classes, D49/1 with piston valves and D49/2 with rotary cam operated Lentz poppet valves. The former were named after shires and the latter after well-known hunts. This interesting picture shows D49/2 No 62756 *The Brocklesby* (a hunt which meets around Grimsby and Brigg) at a picturesque setting in the valley of the River Derwent near Kirkham Abbey with a Scarborough to York train, the sort of job these engines could be found working during most of their lives. All were withdrawn by 1961 but the last survivor, No 62712 *Morayshire*, has most fortuitously been preserved and makes occasional outings over BR lines in Scotland. April 1954. *(J M Jarvis)*
Kodak Retina I 3.5 Ektar Kodachrome 8

Although of alien appearance to LNER devotees, this Ivatt Class 4 2-6-0, which was the last new locomotive type designed for the LMS in 1947, did not come into mainstream production until after nationalisation and BR decided that 77 of the 162 built should be constructed at Darlington and Doncaster. It is appropriate to include a picture of one as they were useful engines on the Eastern Region, not least on the former Midland & Great Northern Joint line and in the north-east of England, as seen here with No 43128 from West Hartlepool shed on the goods avoiding line near Hartlepool station with an up freight train. 21 October 1964. *(Colin Ding)*
Rolleiflex 80mm Planar Agfa CT18 1/500, 5.6

In 1898 Wilson Worsdell introduced to the NER his E1 class shunting 0-6-0Ts. They were similar to his brother Thomas Worsdell's Class E except that the former had wheels 6 in smaller at 4 ft 1¼ in. By the grouping, the class, then known as J72, had risen to 85 and these useful little engines were extensively deployed over the LNER system. Somewhat surprisingly, when Peppercorn modified the scheme Thompson had introduced during World War II to standardise the motive power, this class became the light shunting type and a further 28 were built between 1949 and 1951. Carriage shunting and pilot work at Newcastle Central was regular work for J72s, and No 68723 from Gateshead shed was given special treatment in May 1960 (along with No 68736 at York). Plain black gave way to NER green livery with BR numbers flanked by the BR and NER emblems, as seen here at Central station. A year later No 68736 came up from York to join its green twin until they were both withdrawn in the autumn of 1961. 9 September 1960. *(T B Owen)*
Leica IIIc 50mm Summicron Kodachrome 8 1 sec, f5

Bearing in mind what impressive locomotives Gresley's V2 class were, and that the LNER had an enlightened policy of naming its fleet, it was surprising that only eight out of the class of 184 were named, and one of these, No 60964 *The Durham Light Infantry*, was not so bestowed until it had been in BR ownership for 10 years. However, two of the names made up in words for the numerical lack of names, and No 60809, seen here easing gently through Newcastle Central station with a northbound goods train, was one of them. Its prominent nameplate proclaims *The Snapper, The East Yorkshire Regiment, The Duke of York's Own,* complete with badge and regimental colours painted on the backing plate! The other lengthily-named V2 is illustrated on p11. 2 June 1962. *(Michael Mensing)*
Kodak Retina IIa f2 Xenon Agfa CT18 1/500, f2.4

A wide-angle view of a clean Thompson B1 on shed at Darlington, looking very smart in lined black livery just ex-repairs at the works. No 61013 was one of the small second batch constructed in 1946; by 1950 there were 410. The first 40 were given names of species of antelope, which had the effect of producing some very unfamiliar looking words, including the shortest name on a BR engine — *Gnu*. No 61013 was named *Topi* after a breed of antelope found in East Africa. So christened, and with No 8305 *Bongo* on the GE section (later No 61005), perhaps it was not surprising that with true Cockney wit Stratford men quickly referred to the class as 'bleedin ole Bongos'. Whatever their strange names, the B1s gave good service nearly to the end of steam on the Eastern Region. The last three survivors were withdrawn in June 1967, leaving two in non-revenue departmental service until 1968. Fortunately two, Nos 61264 and 61306, have been preserved. Both are now on the GCR at Loughborough, the latter active and the former undergoing long term restoration. 13 May 1962. (*T B Owen*)
Leica M2   35mm Summicron   Kodachrome II 1/125, f4.5

Another B1 4-6-0, No 61021 *Reitbok* from York shed, in the yard at Pickering shunting the daily pick-up goods from York to Malton and Whitby. From here northwards to Grosmont this former NER line has become the preserved North Yorkshire Moors Railway.

No 61021 was built in 1947 and was withdrawn from York shed when that depot lost its steam allocation in June 1967. 13 April 1964.
(G W Morrison)
Zeiss Contaflex 2.8 Tessar Agfa CT18

Of distinctive appearance, Gresley 0-6-0T J50/4 class No 68984 going about its business shunting at Leeds City station. These engines were designed specifically for use on the steeply-graded lines of the West Riding. A total of 102 locomotives were constructed over a long period between 1913 and 1939, and were widely distributed over the system. This engine was built at Gorton in 1938 and withdrawn in 1963. Seven of the class went into departmental service but these all ceased work in 1965 and none have been preserved. 12 October 1962. *(G W Morrison)*
Zeiss Contaflex 2.8 Tessar Agfa CT18

Like all the major British companies, the LNER had its share of 0-6-0 goods engines and in 1926 Gresley introduced a series with 5 ft 2 in coupled wheels as Class J39. By the time construction had ceased in 1941, 289 had been built making them the most numerous Gresley class and, by coincidence, the same number as the numerically largest LNER pre-grouping class, the GER J15 (see pages 18 and 57). Although designed as goods engines and deployed over nearly all the system; they could also be seen on stopping passenger trains and summer Saturday expresses and extras. This picture portrays a typical duty, showing No 64796, which was built at Darlington in 1929, on a down goods train having just passed Wakefield Westgate station. A little over a year later this engine was withdrawn and the class became extinct. 24 August 1961.

(G W Morrison)

Zeiss Contaflex   2.8 Tessar   Agfa CT18

The clean lines of the Thompson breed is clearly evident in this portrait of O1 class 2-8-0 No 63890 standing outside March shed. These engines were a rebuild of some of the Robinson O4 class which had in effect been the mainstay heavy goods 2-8-0 of the 1920-30s. Thompson's modification to the older engines included the fitting of the No 2 standard boiler (similar to that on the B1s), new cylinders, Walschaerts valve gear and side-window cab. However, the rebuilding programme, which commenced in 1944, was overshadowed by construction of LMS Stanier 8Fs, the LNER's Class O6, and then the purchase of 200 ex-WD Austerities (see page 80), so only 58 were rebuilt at Gorton in the years 1944-49. This engine, built in 1919, was rebuilt in 1946 and withdrawn in 1963. 10 April 1960.
(Norman Glover)
Voigtlander Vito B   50mm Skopar
Kodachrome 8

The railway scene as it used to be in the steam era, with a general view at Spalding, a Fenland market town situated in the centre of the bulb farming region of Lincolnshire. Once a busy station, it had trains radiating in six directions over tracks of the GN, GN & GE Joint and Midland & Great Northern Joint railways. Here B1 No 61073 is waiting to work southwards to Peterborough North with an afternoon local train. 24 June 1961. *(Peter J Coster)* *Periflex 50mm Wray Agfa CT18*

In 1897 Ivatt introduced the first 4-4-0 to the GNR. This was a logical development of that company's earlier Stirling 2-4-0s for use on secondary passenger duties, and 45 engines were built at Doncaster between 1896 and 1899; they eventually became LNER Class D3. In 1944 this engine was selected for hauling Officers' special trains, and for this promotion it was fitted with a new cab with two side windows in place of the rather bare GNR style of the rest of the class, adorned with a brass capped chimney and renumbered 2000 from 4075. It was also given full LNER lined green livery and the tender was painted with the LNER coat of arms flanked by the company initials. This historic picture shows No 2000 in all its glory at Grantham shed where it was stationed for its exalted work. When shopped again in January 1950, it was renumbered 62000 and the BR emblem substituted on the tender, but sadly this did not last long as it was withdrawn in October 1951, the last of the class in service. 26 June 1948. (*J M Jarvis*) *Kodak Retina I   3.5 Ektar   Kodachrome*

Not surprisingly following nationalisation of the LNER in January 1948, the new owners tried out various experimental liveries on different engines, and in June 1948 four Gresley A4s were repainted from the Garter blue livery to a darker shade of blue with red, cream and grey lining. Here is No 60028 *Walter K Whigham* at Grantham in that livery which it carried until 1950 when it was repainted in what had become the standard BR express passenger blue livery with black and white lining. This again was changed in 1952 when No 60028 was painted in the BR Brunswick green livery which was applied to all the class between 1951 and 1953. 26 June 1948. (*J M Jarvis*)

Kodak Retina I   3.5 Ektar   Kodachrome

Vital railway traffic for which the LNER and its successor was and is competently able to handle is the haulage of coal and other bulk commodities. From Rising Sun Colliery at Wallsend near Newcastle upon Tyne, heading tender first out of the setting sun, come J27 No 65812 pulling and K1 No 62062 pushing their load towards the photographer as they reverse up-grade off the colliery branch towards the Percy Main to Blyth line, the K1 then to take the train northwards to Cambois power station. 13 January 1967. *(M J Johnson)*
Leica IIIc   50mm Summitar   Agfa CT18